Reclaim Yo...

SELF LOVE
Made Easy

For The Busy Christian Woman:
Learn to Value Yourself &
See Yourself Through God's Eyes

AMA BREW

Cover design by 100Covers

Edited by Nancee-Laetitia Marin, thelanguageagent.com

Formatted by Jodi Salice, highrealmgraphics.com

Paperback ISBN: 978-1-7358224-3-3
eBook ISBN: 978-1-7358224-4-0

DEDICATION

This book is dedicated to all women who have identified with labels like people pleaser, follower, overachiever, drama queen, sensitive, and doormat at different points in their lives and are looking to increase their self-love and rebuild their self-confidence.

You deserve to have a balanced self-esteem.

TABLE OF CONTENTS

INTRODUCTION

We live in a world where people are labeled based on their actions and behaviors. When a woman shows behaviors outside the norm, others ask her, "What's wrong with you?" When a woman exhibits such behaviors, others give her labels that describe her such as people pleaser, follower, codependent, overachiever, overemotional, drama queen, defensive, and so on.

These labels may genuinely be the perfect description for any woman who exhibits certain deserving characteristic behaviors. However, I believe these labels may identify the symptoms of deeper underlying issues in a woman—lack of self-love and an internal struggle with self-esteem.

When a woman resorts to behaviors such as people pleasing, being emotional and triggered, overperforming, overachieving, and lying to be accepted by others, she may be exhibiting symptoms that may make her unacceptable on the outside, but indeed, it may just be a cry for help. She may just need support for something going on inside that's deeply rooted in a lack of self-love or battered self-esteem.

Yes, I've lived my fair share of those previously mentioned labels. As I journey through life, I've identified with those labels at different stages in my life. And no, I'm not afraid to share my struggles with you because I want you to understand that I'm not coming to you as a woman who hasn't had self-love and self-esteem issues to a considerable degree. I want you to know that I've had my low and high points, and I've been on this journey for many years, so I understand you and hear your struggles too.

If you read my biography at the back of this book, you might think my life looks all perfect, but things aren't as they seem. I want to share my struggles with self-love so you can know that true transformation and success on this journey are possible.

Self-esteem was one of my biggest struggles from my teenage years. I grew up as a fat kid who always got called names and asked why I have a big stomach. Though I was loud and tried to defend myself on the outside, the constant taunts affected how I viewed myself and how I accepted myself deep inside of me. I always wanted to be accepted by others, so I'd inconvenience myself by putting on a façade just to fit in. I'd even come up with stories so I could be deemed acceptable by the people I wanted to be associated with. I'd do anything for external validation and push myself so hard to achieve things so I could be seen and respected.

I moved to France and had the shock of my life. I didn't realize how different I was physically until I kept getting questions about my hair, my skin color, and how I spoke. This deepened my already existing self-consciousness and self-doubt. I always felt like the odd one out in the room, not because I wasn't good enough internally or smart enough, but because I felt different. I felt like something was wrong with me. In that environment, I always had an influx of thoughts about not being good enough and not being lovable. Simply put, I started secretly yearning to be like others, to be accepted by them, and to fit in with them. Exactly what I'd battled with as a teenager came back to me but this time in a more profound way and for reasons beyond my control—my skin color and hair type.

Then an opportunity came for me to move to the US. When I moved to the US, I felt accepted and at home. I felt like I could finally fit in. And yes, that was true until I got pregnant with my daughter and my body started changing.

From that point onward, I went into a downward spiral of negative thoughts about myself and my body. I just couldn't love myself anymore. This new mommy body was freaking me out. By this point, my self-esteem issues were not centered on my skin color, my hair texture, or how smart I was. It was centered on the stretch marks on my tummy, the C-section scar, my sagging breasts, and the ever-changing pigmentation on my skin due to hormonal imbalances that had developed from my pregnancy.

One day, as I reflected on life, I wondered why I was constantly in a struggle with my self-esteem. Why did I keep identifying with labels like people pleaser, follower, codependent, overachiever, overemotional, and drama queen? Why was I constantly entangled in toxic relationships and social engagements? Why did my self-esteem keep fluctuating from high to low? Why was it hard for me to accept myself sometimes? Why was I always trying too hard for people to like and accept me? These questions flooded my mind. They led me to a journey of finding a solid, nonfluctuating way of defining my self-esteem. Along this journey, I discovered more about self-love and self-esteem that I believe will be helpful to you, my dear reader, as you go through your own self-love journey.

Maybe you're just like me. You picked up this book because you've had your own struggle with self-love, self-esteem, and self-worth. Maybe you keep going through highs and lows, and you value yourself in different ways depending on what you're going through at a particular time. Maybe others have constantly given you the previously mentioned labels, or you've identified with those labels. Maybe you've struggled with body dissatisfaction and can't seem to figure out how to place more value on yourself and love yourself.

If you're looking for a solid way of loving yourself and placing value on yourself, then this book is for you. If you want to love yourself and accept yourself irrespective of your challenges, flaws, weaknesses, and trials, then this book is for you. In this book I'll be sharing with you simple truths you can apply to your life so you can develop a balanced self-esteem and begin to see yourself as God sees you.

My prayer is that this book will give you the resources you need to press on toward the goal of developing a solid self-esteem and self-value built on who God says you are.

HOW TO USE THIS BOOK

This book is a three-part book. In the first part, we'll delve into the ins and outs of self-love.

The second part gives strategies for building a balanced self-esteem and beginning to see yourself as God sees you. This part is your toolbox on your self-love journey. The third part helps you jump-start your self-love journey no matter where you are on your journey. There are thought-provoking journal questions at different points in this book to help you do your own introspection as you read.

You may feel overwhelmed by all the material and resources shared, but you don't need to implement them all. Some of the material may apply to you now. Some may be relevant later as you continue your journey. So don't feel pressured to have to implement everything. If you consciously and consistently apply the knowledge in this book to your daily life, you'll reap long-term benefits that will transform your life.

Part One

THE INS AND OUTS OF SELF-LOVE

We'll explore the ins and outs of self-love: the meaning of self-love, the balanced self-esteem, and the importance of developing a balanced self-esteem.

Chapter One

SELF-LOVE IS NOT SELFISH

Love your neighbor as yourself. - Matthew 22:39

I gave a talk at a gathering of Christian women on the topic of self-love. After my presentation, one of the ladies raised her hand and asked me the simple question, "Is self-love selfish?"

I validated her question and inquired about what informed her question. She opened up to the whole group about how she grew up in a community where she was told to show love to others and always put herself last in everything. She explained that she saw herself as an afterthought because she always wanted to please everyone. She even used labels like people pleaser, yes-woman, and codependent to describe herself. To her, being everything for everyone made her more of a virtuous woman, though deep inside of her, sometimes she felt overstretched and taken for granted. She just couldn't speak up because she didn't want to be perceived as an unloving woman. She was inconveniencing herself and unloving to herself so she could be perceived as a good woman.

As she expressed her sentiments and elaborated on her question, the words that kept running through my head was love your neighbors as yourself:

"Teacher, which is the most important commandment in the law of Moses?" Jesus replied, "'You must love the Lord your God with all your heart, all your soul, and all your mind.' This is the first and greatest commandment. A second is equally important: 'Love your neighbor as yourself.'" (Matthew 22:36–39)

Yes, Jesus told his disciples that the greatest commandment is to love God first and the second is to love our neighbors as we love ourselves. He didn't say love God first, then your neighbor, and then yourself.

My understanding of this verse is that our love for God must be the ultimate, followed by our love for ourselves and others. Our love for ourselves is to be just like our love for others. Both of them are on the same pedestal. Love yourself and love others the same way you love yourself. I believe this is a very simple and clear commandment. However, like the lady who shared her experience with the group, many of us were brought up to put ourselves last.

You may be feeling like self-love is selfish. You may have been taught to put yourself last in everything you do. Showing love to humanity starts on the inside. You start with yourself first before you even try to extend it out to others. We have to be kind and patient with ourselves first even before we think about spreading patience and kindness to others. Yes, you have to love yourself first before loving others on the same level you love yourself.

Selfishness is loving yourself only and not spreading that love to others. That breeds pride, egocentric ideologies, and conceitedness. Yes, self-love without consideration of others and extending that love to them is selfish. But self-love that's spread to others at the same level is obedience to the second most important commandment: first love yourself, then love your neighbor as you love yourself.

But many of us women are so busy trying to show love to our world first even before we think about showing love to ourselves. I'm sorry to say we've got it all wrong. And this is why it's so hard to love and walk in the biblical love because we don't even know how that feels and how to do it for ourselves.

You can't give out what you don't have. You can't pour love from an empty love cup. You need to fill yourself and your love cup first even before you try to tip your cup over and pour love to others. First love yourself, then give out that love to others.

"LOVE IS PATIENT AND KIND. LOVE IS NOT JEALOUS OR BOASTFUL OR PROUD OR RUDE. IT DOES NOT DEMAND ITS OWN WAY. IT IS NOT IRRITABLE, AND IT KEEPS NO RECORD OF BEING WRONGED. IT DOES NOT REJOICE ABOUT INJUSTICE BUT REJOICES WHENEVER THE TRUTH WINS OUT. LOVE NEVER GIVES UP, NEVER LOSES FAITH, IS ALWAYS HOPEFUL, AND ENDURES THROUGH EVERY CIRCUMSTANCE."
1 CORINTHIANS 13:4–7

How about you? Start with yourself. You deserve your own love. You deserve to pamper yourself. You deserve to be kind and compassionate to yourself. You deserve to respect yourself. You deserve to be patient with yourself. You deserve to forgive yourself. You deserve not to give up on yourself. You deserve to be hopeful about yourself and your struggles. You deserve to forgive yourself for your past mistakes. You deserve all these attributes of love.

This book helps you love yourself first. I'm so passionate about this book because I want you, my reader, to change your negative idea surrounding self-love. I'm not bringing you information that will make you egoistic.

I'm not bringing you information that will make you proud and conceited. Rather, the purpose of this book is to help you love yourself so much that you can spread genuine love to everyone around you and to the world out there.

Journal Activity

What does self-love mean to me?

_____

_____

_____

_____

_____

_____

_____

_____

Do I believe self-love is not selfish?

_____

_____

_____

_____

_____

_____

_____

_____

_____

Chapter Two
WHAT DO YOU SEE IN THE MIRROR?

When you look in the mirror, what do you see? I'm not just talking about the physical image you see in the mirror. I'm talking more about the mental image that you have of yourself. This mental image is what we call your self-image. Self-image is the way we see ourselves. It's the mental picture we have about ourselves.

Your self-image is important because it affects your attitude toward yourself, your family, your friends, your work, and your chances of success. People who have poor self-image have problems relating to others. We must not think poorly of ourselves, nor must we be proud or conceited. Neither of these attitudes brings happiness, inner fulfillment, and right relationships. God wants us to have a proper self-image. He wants us to think rightly about ourselves. The mental image that you have of yourself goes a long way to affect your self-esteem.

Self-Esteem

Self-esteem is the value that you place on yourself as a woman. So, as a woman, do you value yourself? Do you think you're valuable? Do you think you're good enough? Do you think you're a woman who's not worthy? Do you think you're not valuable or there's nothing good about you? Those feelings you have about yourself have to do with your self-esteem.

Your self-esteem is very important. It has to do with your view of yourself and affects how you treat yourself, how you allow other people to treat you, your behavioral patterns, your self-confidence, and your success in life because it has to do with your view of yourself. If you have disregard for yourself, you're susceptible to depression and low motivation. Too much self-love can also make you proud, conceited, and unlikely to accept mistakes and humbly learn from others.

The way you view yourself affects your output, how you react in situations, and how you allow people to react toward you and to treat you. So your self-esteem is very important. I always say it's the invisible thing affecting the success, productivity, and wellness of a lot of women because sometimes we don't place enough value on ourselves. And sometimes we don't love ourselves enough. We're busy trying to love other people instead of loving ourselves first. So our self-esteem is very, very important.

Two Types of Women

In my quest to understand self-esteem and self-love, I realized there are typically two extreme types of women in relation to self-esteem. As you read about these two sides, I urge you to ask yourself how much you identify with any of what I'm sharing with you.

The Superior Self-Lover

"BECAUSE OF THE PRIVILEGE AND AUTHORITY GOD HAS GIVEN ME, I GIVE EACH OF YOU THIS WARNING: DON'T THINK YOU ARE BETTER THAN YOU REALLY ARE. BE HONEST IN YOUR EVALUATION OF YOURSELVES, MEASURING YOURSELVES BY THE FAITH GOD HAS GIVEN US."

- ROMANS 12:3

Miss Jay is a high achiever who on the outside seems to be soaring. She shows up as the person who has it all together. She's very successful, very driven, and goal oriented in her career.

Life seems good on the outside for her, but she does have her own struggles and flaws. She's not perfect as she portrays herself to be. She's very condescending, and feels she is better than everyone else. Her sense of pride and her hyperfocus on her strengths makes it hard for others to keep a conversation going with her, as they usually feel talked down to. Miss Jay does this without even realizing it. This attitude of hers makes her wonder why people who get closer to her keep withdrawing. As much as she's successful, she feels lonely because she can't seem to make and keep meaningful connections for the long term.

Miss Jay is the typical example of the superior self-lover. The superior self-lover is the woman who is hyperfocused on her strengths. She feels she has no flaws or limitations. Usually, this woman has a superiority complex. Such women are usually perceived as proud and conceited because they talk down to others to make them feel inferior.

The Inferior Self-Lover

Lady Bee is a woman who has so many great things going for her. She excels in her career. She also has kids and a thriving relationship with her husband. She has many talents and inner qualities. However, she's so miserable because she can't see the goodness of God in her life. She's always focused on her shortfalls and her failures. She's so stuck in her past mistakes and always crawling into her shell in social situations because she's afraid she may make a mistake or will be perceived as a flawed woman by the people around her. This is really inhibiting her from living her best life. She constantly needs reassurance from her family and support system and sometimes feels less confident about her decisions and goals in life.

Lady Bee is a typical example of a woman with an inferiority complex. This is the woman hyperfocused on her limitations and problems. She doesn't see anything good about herself. She can't recognize her abilities and her strengths. She also feels less than other people. She always feels like she's not good enough and lovable, and nothing good can come out of it. She has low self-esteem and self-worth.

Causes of Low Self-Esteem

There are different causes of low self-esteem. If a woman grows up in a family that has a practice of disapproval, this can follow the woman into her adulthood and make her develop a low self-esteem. Also, growing up in a physically or emotionally abusive home can cause childhood trauma that can lead a woman to doubt herself, her worth, and her value. Low self-esteem can also be caused by a poor school environment or a toxic or dysfunctional workplace in which a person is constantly micromanaged and criticized for their shortfalls. Cycles of abusive relationships can also lead to poor self-esteem. When a woman is constantly being told she's not good enough by an abusive partner, she may start believing what the abuser is saying about her and develop low self-esteem and consequently an inferiority complex. Facing discrimination of any kind can lead to low self-esteem. This can make a person feel there's something wrong with them and constantly doubt and look down on themselves.

The Struggle Is Real

My dear reader, you are not alone. I must be honest with you—I've found myself fluctuating between these two kinds of women at different points in my life depending on what I'm going through, my sense of self-awareness, and where my focus is. I've been in cycles where I overstretch myself and achieve big things that inflate my self-esteem until something bad happens, and then I sink down to the lower end of the spectrum. The struggle is real. That's why I'm so eager to share with you some more about balanced self-esteem and how we can achieve that sense of inner balance irrespective of circumstances at any given point in time. In the next chapters we'll explore more about balanced self-esteem and how you can achieve it

Journal Activity

Which of these women do you identify with?

_____

_____

_____

_____

_____

_____

_____

_____

_____

_____

_____

_____

_____

_____

_____

_____

_____

_____

_____

Chapter Three

BALANCED SELF-ESTEEM

Then God said, "Let us make human beings in our image, to be like us. They will reign over the fish in the sea, the birds in the sky, the livestock, all the wild animals on the earth, and the small animals that scurry along the ground."

So God created human beings in his own image. In the image of God he created them; male and female he created them.

Then God blessed them and said, "Be fruitful and multiply. Fill the earth and govern it. Reign over the fish in the sea, the birds in the sky, and all the animals that scurry along the ground." - Genesis 1:26–28

The above verse of the Scriptures is one of my favorites. I love it because it explains the reason and purpose of our existence here on earth as human beings. It's the fundamental truth of why God created us in the first place.

Yes, God made us—male and female. He first created us in his image to be like him. He created us to have dominion over everything else on earth. He then blessed us and told us to be fruitful and productive and reign over everything. Wow! We're like little gods here on earth, created for a purpose. What's more, God's creation wasn't complete until he created the woman. We're not an afterthought. We're what he needed to complete everything he'd made. Without us, men wouldn't feel complete, and God wouldn't feel like his work of creation was done. This shows us how valuable women are to the world.

Oftentimes, we totally forget the basic reason why God made us. We get caught up in everyday life challenges and stressors to the point where we lose focus of the fundamental reason and purpose of our existence. I'm definitely so guilty of this, and as I write this chapter, I'm having a very big aha moment.

I am asking myself, "Why do I always forget these insights about why God made me and the authority he gave me when he made me in the moments when I truly need it?" I guess it makes sense because when we're going through stressful things, we go into stress response or fight-or-flight mode, which makes it hard for us to rationalize and think about fundamental and simple truths like "I am made in the image of God, and I have a purpose and dominion here on earth."

My dear reader, you are valuable with or without your weaknesses. You are valuable no matter what you are going through presently or have been through in the past. You are valuable no matter what mistakes you made in the past. You are valuable no matter your achievements or success in life. This may be hard to believe, but it's the truth based on what the word of God tells us about who we are. Your weaknesses don't determine your value. You are valuable because you are made in the image of God, and God has a purpose for your life.

No one person is more important than others in the sight of God, and no one person is less than the other. We are all equal and worthy except that we all have different characteristics. I always say our Creator is the most creative personality who has ever existed because he made us all unique. It's important to recognize this truth, as it helps us rid ourselves of the fear of being less than others and being unacceptable.

The Balanced Self-Lover

Before I explain to you the meaning of the term balanced self-esteem, I want to introduce you to Miss Vera, a very good friend of mine. She's a woman who excels at what she does. She's very self-aware. She capitalizes on many of her great strengths for maximum success. She has grown to understand herself and who she is as a person. She knows she's not perfect. She acknowledges her weaknesses. She sees her weaknesses as an opportunity for growth and is constantly working on becoming a better person. However, as she goes on this journey to betterment, she still loves herself and values who she is on the inside. She's so open to constructive criticism and looks for opportunities to learn new things.

Miss Vera is a typical example of a woman with a balanced self-esteem who I call the balanced self-lover. The balanced self-lover is the woman who has a balanced view of herself and who she is as a person. She's come to realize that she has her own unique sets of skills, talents, and limitations. At the end of the day, she's not a perfect person, but she's valuable. She's the woman who's able to recognize that she's not perfect, as no one is perfect. She's able to accept herself for who she is, including her strengths and limitations.

The term balanced self-esteem is a term I love very much. Like Miss Vera, the poster child of balanced self-esteem, a woman with a balanced self-esteem has a healthy way of viewing herself and her worth. A balanced self-esteem is your ability to capitalize on your strengths, work on the weaknesses you can overcome, and live with a notion that though you have limitations, you are valuable, period.

A balanced self-esteem is having a healthy dose of high and low self-worth. It's the ability to recognize the difference between arrogance and confidence. A woman with a balanced self-esteem isn't afraid of constructive feedback. She's not afraid to say no and set boundaries. She doesn't try to please people and be liked by everyone. She's firm, assertive, and not afraid to voice her needs and express herself. She doesn't try to be perfect but puts in her best in everything she does, capitalizes on her strengths for success, and isn't afraid of making mistakes.

THREE TYPES OF WOMEN

	Inferior Self-Lover	Balanced Self-Lover	Superior Self-Lover
Focus	Hyperfocused on weaknesses	Balanced view of herself including strengths & weaknesses	Hyperfocused on her strengths
Respect	Looks down on herself	Respects everyone including herself	Looks down on other people
Labels	Inferiority complex, low self-esteem	Confident, assertive	Superiority complex, proud
Self-Worth	Unhealthy dose of low self-worth	Healthy amount of low and high self-worth	Unhealthy dose of high self-worth

www.empoweredforbalance.com

You may be asking, "Ama, why is it even necessary to do all this inner work on self-esteem and developing a balanced self-esteem?" The truth is that this is very important. If you have low disregard for yourself, you're susceptible to depression and low drive and motivation. Too much self-love can also make you pompous, and unlikely to accept mistakes and humbly learn from others. In the next chapter, I'm going to share with you the benefits and importance of developing a balanced self-esteem.

Journal Activity

What does balanced self-esteem mean to you?

_____

_____

_____

_____

_____

_____

_____

_____

_____

_____

_____

_____

_____

_____

_____

_____

_____

_____

_____

Chapter Four

WHY DO YOU NEED A BALANCED SELF-ESTEEM?

In this chapter I'm going to help you understand the importance of developing a balanced self-esteem and becoming a balanced self-lover. Yes, that's exactly who I want to be, and I hope I can convince you to aim at becoming a balanced self-lover too.

Stand Up for Yourself

I remember the many times I said yes to things that genuinely did not sit well with me. My favorite statement was "I'm good" or "You're good." I'd smile through these words, but genuinely, deep inside of me I wasn't okay, let alone good. I'd constantly go all out saying yes to things and compromising my deep-seated needs and convictions. When there was no reciprocity, I'd feel resentful. The resentment in my heart was from the fact that I expected others to do what I did—inconvenience themselves for me. The truth was that they weren't even aware I was inconveniencing myself for them, so they were unaware of my expectations of them.

I also always took on more than I could handle because I was busy saying yes to everyone and piling on top of my schedule things I definitely knew I wouldn't be able to handle, consequently leading to cycles of chronic stress, overwhelm, and burnout.

I must say that acknowledging my worth gave me the confidence to express myself and stand up for myself. My journey to becoming a balanced self-lover is helping me change the trajectory of being a people pleaser to becoming assertive and not afraid to say no.

Many times, as women, we find it difficult to say no and stand up for ourselves because we're afraid of what people will say when we truly express ourselves assertively. We take on more than we can handle and keep inconveniencing ourselves because we're not confident enough to express ourselves assertively.

Assertiveness is one of the benefits of becoming a balanced self-lover. With a healthy and balanced self-esteem, you're more likely to be assertive in expressing your needs and opinions. You're your biggest advocate. No one will advocate for you as much as you can advocate for yourself. When you have a balanced self-esteem, you're able to advocate for yourself and not allow others to take advantage of you. It's a lot easier to speak up for yourself if you have balanced self-esteem and know your worth. Yes, becoming a balanced self-lover affects how you allow others to treat you.

Make Bold Decisions

Oh dear, another thing that comes to my mind as I write this chapter is the number of times I second-guessed myself over simple choices—small everyday decisions like what to wear, what to eat, and what to do. Low self-esteem can really make life decisions very difficult. Second-guessing becomes your best friend. Another thing that shows up is fear of the consequences of your decisions. "What if?" becomes your favorite question. "What if I am wrong? What if no one likes it? What if I'm embarrassed?" Low self-esteem causes a lot of self-doubt, anxiety, and negative self-talk.

You always skip to the worst-case scenario because you're not confident in yourself and the ability to make the right choices. When you have a balanced self-esteem, you're confident in your choices. Understanding yourself, being self-aware, and knowing what defines you— your strengths, abilities, weaknesses, and strengths—

empower you to make the right decisions and choices in life. That's what it means to be a balanced self-lover.

Form Secure and Honest Relationships

A balanced self-esteem increases your ability to form secure and honest relationships. When you become a balanced self-lover, you know your worth, and you're not afraid to show up as your true self. You're also less likely to stay in unhealthy, abusive relationships that violate your boundaries and disrespect you.

With a low self-esteem, you may put on a mask just to keep up appearances and be accepted by people. This makes people fall in love with you for what you show up as instead of who you really are. What usually happens is that the true you definitely shows through the mask, eventually either embarrassing you or making people perceive you as fake.

Becoming a balanced self-lover also affects how you treat others. If you have a balanced view of yourself, you can see all people as valuable, and thus you treat them with respect and esteem. You can value people's strengths. You can create realistic expectations of others, realizing that no one is perfect. This makes you less likely to be overly critical of others.

In addition to this, becoming a balanced self-lover allows you to be less critical of yourself. When you're less critical of yourself, you can value yourself despite your shortcomings and weaknesses. You feel you're worthy of respect and proper treatment from others. You don't put up with disrespect from others. You give yourself grace for your mistakes. When you show yourself compassion, you're less likely to be too hard on yourself.

In short, a balanced self-esteem affects how you treat yourself, how you allow others to treat you, and helps you be less critical of others.

Become More Resilient

There are four different seasons in most North American regions. Summer is my daughter's favorite time of the year. When it's sunny and warm out, we can go out and have fun in nature—at the beach or at the lake. After summer comes fall, my favorite time of the year. I get to see some of the best fall foliage in the country. The leaves turn orange, and then come the pumpkins and Thanksgiving. Fall is a time of harvest. One of my favorite fall drinks is warm apple cider. After fall comes winter. Honestly, I really hate winter. I was born in a very hot tropical climate. As much as I've been living here in the New England region for more than eight years, I still haven't adjusted. I get so cold, and I still can't believe the amount of snow that falls here. After winter comes spring. All the snow melts. Plants and flowers start to bloom again. Every year, as we go through the change in seasons, I tell myself there's time for everything, and life has its seasons. There's time for sowing, time for watering, and time for harvesting.

As women, we go through different seasons and times. There are happy times and hard times. One thing I know for sure is that life happens and trials happen. Happy times are usually easy to deal with because they involve pleasant experiences. The biggest challenge is when hard times hit us. How do we weather the storm? Can we bounce back after going through hard times? When bad days come, having a solid self-esteem is vital in weathering the storm.

A person with low self-esteem may find it hard to bounce back from a setback. A balanced self-lover will realize that this is a bad day and what she's going through doesn't define her self-esteem. Her self-esteem won't be affected by the season she's in. This gives her more confidence to weather the bad storms. A balanced self-esteem makes you resilient and better able to withstand stress, trials, setbacks, and challenges.

Practice Self-Care

When you have a balanced self-esteem, you're more likely to practice proper self-care. One thing I always say is that what we value is what we take care of. That's why it's so easy for us to care for our most expensive possessions. When you develop balanced self-esteem, it's so easy for you to take care of yourself and nurture your wellness.

Self-care starts with self-value and self-esteem. You will make time for yourself if you have a balanced self-esteem. You won't be afraid to pay and invest in yourself and your health if you have a balanced self-esteem. You won't be afraid to enforce your mental, emotional, and physical boundaries if you have a balanced self-esteem. This has a long-term effect on your level of burnout and stress.

Becoming a balanced self-lover makes it easy for you to care for yourself physically, mentally and emotionally.

Success and Confidence in Life

Your self-esteem affects your self-confidence and success in life. A woman with a low self-esteem has lower motivation and may be less likely to try new things and strive for her goals and vision.

A balanced self-lover usually has the drive to try new things. She has the motivation to keep pushing even when things are hard. She sees her strengths, opportunities, abilities, and talents. She recognizes what she has and capitalizes on that for success. She's not fixated on her weakness. She works toward improving those weaknesses and doesn't give up when things don't turn out as she expects. A balanced self-esteem also makes you more likely to accept criticism and learn from it. A balanced self-esteem makes you more open to humble yourself and learn from others.

WRAP-UP

We've covered balanced self-esteem in this chapter by clarifying that self-love is not selfish and explaining what self-image is—the mental image we have of ourselves, which affects our self-esteem. We've also discussed the two extreme types of women in relation to self-esteem. Finally, I've explained to you what it means to be a balanced self-lover and the importance of becoming a balanced self-lover.

My aim in this chapter is to let you see the benefits of developing a balanced self-esteem and becoming a balanced self-lover. I hope that I've accomplished my mission and you're now even more motivated to start or continue your journey to self-love. Perhaps you may be saying, "Ama, you've really convinced me about the importance of developing a balanced self-esteem. I really want to become a balanced self-lover, but I don't know how to do that or where to even start." Or perhaps you see and understand what it means to be a balanced self-lover, but you feel it's unrealistic and out of your reach. Don't worry. I've got you. The following chapters will show you how to become a balanced self-lover. Just keep reading on to learn the keys and strategies for improving your self-esteem and becoming a balanced self-lover.

Part Two

HOW TO DEVELOP A BALANCED SELF-ESTEEM

I'll share with you how you can develop a balanced self-image and begin to see yourself as God sees you. This part will elaborate on the keys I've been implementing on my own self-love journey and in my work with my coaching clients, which has created significant progress and results in my clients' lives and mine.

Chapter Five

ACCEPT YOUR UNIQUENESS

A spiritual gift is given to each of us so we can help each other. To one person the Spirit gives the ability to give wise advice; to another the same Spirit gives a message of special knowledge. The same Spirit gives great faith to another, and to someone else the one Spirit gives the gift of healing. He gives one person the power to perform miracles, and another the ability to prophesy. He gives someone else the ability to discern whether a message is from the Spirit of God or from another spirit. Still another person is given the ability to speak in unknown languages, while another is given the ability to interpret what is being said. It is the one and only Spirit who distributes all these gifts. He alone decides which gift each person should have.
—1 Corinthians 12:7-11

On the Empowered for Balance podcast, I've had the opportunity to interact with women from all over the world. One thing I know for sure is that these women are similar in some ways, but each one of these women is different in her own way. None of them is exactly the same.

As women are made in the image of God and given the mandate to subdue the earth and be fruitful, God has given every one of us different characteristics and gifts, which I call our unique specs. I always say unique specs are your specific characteristics, particularly as a woman. These characteristics include your physical appearance. Every single woman is different in how she looks. We all have physical peculiarities related to our skin tone, hair texture, eye color, height, weight, muscle tone—just to mention a few. These elements form our physical specifications. Mentally, we also have our unique capacities and ways of reasoning. Emotionally, we're all different. Our behaviors are also different. We all have different temperaments, not to mention our talents, gifts, abilities, and strengths. All these elements come together to form your unique specs and who you are as a person.

In addition to your personal characteristics, there are some environmental characteristics that add up to and influence your unique specs. These include your family of origin, the community you were raised in and its culture, the schools you attended, and the teachers you interacted with. Every person on earth has a unique spec.

To become a balanced self-lover, you need to change your distorted self-perception and accept your unique specs. You need to realize that you are who you are and have the characteristics you have because you're unique. There's no one on earth like you. In some ways you're different, but in many ways you're similar to others.

We have been given the characteristics and gifts we have so we can fulfill our unique purpose here on earth. As mentioned in the beginning of this book, remember that the greater purpose of humanity is to be fruitful and multiply. All of us have a part to play in this great purpose, and the unique specs we have individually is exactly what we need to fulfill our part in this greater mission. So the earlier you can accept your uniqueness, the better it will be for you, enabling you to develop a balanced self-esteem and feel empowered to fulfill your purpose here on earth.

You're not weird. You're not odd. You're not an outlier. You're not unacceptable just because you aren't like others. You're indeed special and have a special purpose here on earth. Just embrace your uniqueness and depend on God to use that uniqueness for his glory to fulfill your mission here on earth.

Chapter Six

CULTURE IS JUST A GUIDE

A lady reached out to me the other day on social media via direct message. She expressed interest in chatting with me about a vital issue. I invited her to a free strategy session with me, which I usually offer to my clients. In that session she shared her frustrations of being a late bloomer and failing as a woman. Tears streamed down her face for almost five minutes nonstop.

As I sat and listened to her, my heart really sank. Tears also welled up in my eyes. She finally let it all out and had the strength to share more. "Ama, I'm from a culture where certain milestones have been put in place. A woman must get married by the age of thirty and have kids by thirty-two. In addition to this milestone, a woman must not only have kids, but specifically, she must also give birth to a son who'll be the next of kin to his dad. If a woman has only daughters, she's considered unproductive. Some families who are very vested in this cultural standard may sometimes look for a different woman to birth a male child for their sons because they want their family names to live on and they need the next of kin to their sons."

She sniffled between words, but she tried to regain her composure so she could continue to talk to me. "I'm such a failure. I'm twenty-nine years old, and there's no sign of a man, let alone pregnancy and a son."

I asked her, "Aside from this very important milestone that you feel you've failed at, what are some other things you've been able to achieve in your twenty-nine-year life journey?"

She answered, "I've completed my master's degree, I have a very stable income, and I've just moved into my new home that I just bought. I can afford everything I want. I have good friends, and I belong to a supportive church family. But despite all these, I still feel incomplete and like a failure. My parents can't have a conversation with me without bringing up this issue of marriage. Ama, I've failed. I'm not woman enough . . . "

I could hear the defeat in her voice and see it written all over her face as she poured her heart out to me. After the session, I sat in front of my computer, deep in thought for close to an hour. I realized how societal standards and cultural milestones are creating a sense of unworthiness for a lot of women. I realized how much I could identify with this pressure to fit into societal expectations. Sometimes our church culture also creates some of these expectations. We're trying so hard to live up to them to the point where we can't acknowledge all the good things we're winning at.

My dear reader, maybe you're like my client. You grew up in a culture with strict milestones and standards that have been set for women. Maybe you don't feel valuable because you can't live up to your cultural and societal norms. Maybe you feel under pressure to perform and show up in a certain way that your culture expects of you, and this has made you so unfulfilled and unhappy inside.

My social studies teacher taught me that culture is the way of life of a group of people. There are so many cultures in this world, and each culture has what defines it. I've had the opportunity to live on three different continents and experience the cultures of all these places. I must tell you that each of these cultures have some similarities but more differences as to what they expect from women. With this in mind, I've come to the conclusion that there's no such thing as a perfect woman because every culture has its definition of a perfect woman. These societal norms only serve as a guide but shouldn't be used to define your worth as a woman.

I want to reassure you today that you haven't failed as a woman. You haven't failed just because you can't match up to the image and expectation that your culture has set for you. First of all, please stop defining your worth by cultural standards. Stop placing value on yourself based on how much you've been able to achieve what your culture expects of you. You may not have been able to live up to exactly what your culture expects of you, but you'll be surprised that where you are in life now and who you are as a person may be considered perfect in a different culture.

As you go on this journey to becoming a balanced self-lover, please shift from defining your worth by what your culture expects of you. See culture as a guide and not the ultimate qualification for defining who a good woman is.

Journal Activity

How am I defining my self worth by
cultural and societal norms?

_____

_____

_____

_____

_____

_____

_____

_____

_____

_____

_____

_____

_____

_____

_____

_____

_____

_____

_____

Chapter Seven

STOP DEFINING YOUR SELF-ESTEEM BY EXTERNAL FACTORS

"What is the price of five sparrows—two copper coins? Yet God does not forget a single one of them. And the very hairs on your head are all numbered. So don't be afraid; you are more valuable to God than a whole flock of sparrows."

—Luke 12:6-7

The next key to developing a balanced self-esteem is to stop defining your self-esteem by external factors. We live in a world where people classify others based on external factors. People are treated with respect depending on how much wealth or worldly things they may have. This has led many women to define their worth on how many of these external factors they can boast about.

Some of my biggest discoveries on my journey to becoming a balanced self-lover are the consequences of defining my self-esteem by external factors. I realized I had fluctuating self-esteem that swung high or low depending on what was going on externally at a particular point in time.

Maybe your self-esteem goes up when you have all the things you want or all the things society wants you to have. Then it goes down when you don't have them or when things aren't going well. External factors do change. Situations change. Pandemics happen. Accidents happen. Life happens. But even in the midst of everything, you're still valuable. It doesn't matter if you're healthy or sick, rich or poor, slim or fat, married or unmarried, with children or childless, a homeowner or homeless. Remember that God created you in his image and for a purpose. That's why you're going to have a solid and unshakable self-esteem no matter what happens. You're not going to define your worth by what's going on on the outside but rather about who you are as a person and who you are inside of you.

Journal Activity

*What external factors am I using
to define my self-worth?*

_____

_____

_____

_____

_____

_____

_____

_____

_____

_____

_____

_____

_____

_____

_____

_____

_____

_____

_____

_____

Chapter Eight

DEFINE YOUR SELF-ESTEEM BY WHO GOD SAYS YOU ARE

"I knew you before I formed you in your mother's womb. Before you were born I set you apart and appointed you as my prophet to the nations."

—Jeremiah 1:5

When Steve Jobs and his two friends created Apple, they were the only ones who could tell the world what it was worth and what it was made for. When Elon Musk created Tesla, he was the only one who could tell the world the value of his invention, its price, and what it was made for.

Christian Louboutin created the red bottoms we women love so much. The creator of those beautiful but pricey shoes knew the class and value his shoes had and named his price. Of course, those who see that value still purchase those shoes. There have been some Louboutin knockoffs, but those are so cheap and can't be sold at the price point of the originals.

All I'm trying to say here is that you were also created. You didn't just happen by accident. You may have thought you were an accident. Your parents may have thought so too. But God knows why he made the egg from your mom and that single sperm out of the millions from your dad to create you and have you grow in your mom's womb until you were finally born into this world.

With this in mind, the best person to tell you who you are and what you are worth is God. The world may classify you in a certain group because of external reasons. However, God is the one who can help you see your value.

He says he knew you even when you were in your mother's womb, and he knows the thoughts and plans he has for you. He created you for a specific purpose that only you can bring into this world. He's the only one who can tell you who you are and what purpose he has for you.

You can't have a solid self-esteem until you turn inward, look above to the heavens, and see yourself as God sees you. It wasn't the case for me until I realized I was making the same mistake over and over again. At every phase in my life when I transitioned out of my comfort zone, I defined my self-esteem by external circumstances and things. Then one day I chanced on Matthew 7:24–27:

"ANYONE WHO LISTENS TO MY TEACHING AND FOLLOWS IT IS WISE, LIKE A PERSON WHO BUILDS A HOUSE ON SOLID ROCK. THOUGH THE RAIN COMES IN TORRENTS AND THE FLOODWATERS RISE AND THE WINDS BEAT AGAINST THAT HOUSE, IT WON'T COLLAPSE BECAUSE IT IS BUILT ON BEDROCK. BUT ANYONE WHO HEARS MY TEACHING AND DOESN'T OBEY IT IS FOOLISH, LIKE A PERSON WHO BUILDS A HOUSE ON SAND. WHEN THE RAINS AND FLOODS COME AND THE WINDS BEAT AGAINST THAT HOUSE, IT WILL COLLAPSE WITH A MIGHTY CRASH."

This is a verse that I've seen over and over again. We even sang about it in Sunday school. But this time I had a very different understanding of this same verse.

I realized that I needed to base my self-value and self-love on the word of God and what the Bible says about me as a person. I realized that my source of self-value and self-esteem must be from God, be rooted in what he says I am, and who he has destined me to be. I realized that if my self-esteem is built on this solid rock, no matter what comes my way—bad days, trials, temptations, illnesses, or pandemics—my self-esteem will not be moved because it will be like the house built on solid rock. The rains came and beat it, but it didn't collapse. This was a big eye opener for me on my self-love journey. It made me realize I had it wrong the whole time.

There are so many Bible verses that talk about how important you are as a woman and your value here on earth. The Bible says you have peace with God (Romans 5:1). You are accepted by God (Ephesians 1:6). You are a child of God (John 1:12). You are tenderly loved (John 3:16). You are the aroma of Christ to God (2 Corinthians 2:15). You are the temple of God (1 Corinthians 3:16). You have your needs met by God (Philippians 4:19).

So stop seeking external validation because that's not solid. People can always change their opinions about you. Systems and cultures always change and have a collective approach to classifying you. But only God sees your individuality and looks beyond your past mistakes and your negatives. Only God and his word can give you a genuine evaluation of your worth and value here on earth.

Chapter Nine

FORGIVE YOURSELF FOR PAST MISTAKES

But if we confess our sins to him, he is faithful and just to forgive us our sins and to cleanse us from all wickedness.

—1 John 1:9

Forgiving your past is vital in your ability to develop a balanced self-esteem. Some of the biggest damages I did to myself was holding on to my past mistakes and allowing the guilt from my past to stop me from loving myself and placing value on myself. I grew up in a very conservative Christian culture where judgment was preached to me over and over again. My Sunday school teacher did a good job on making me realize the importance of making responsible choices and realizing the consequences of everything I do.

I was taught that sin is not good and living in sin will lead me to hell where I'll burn for eternity. However, living in righteousness gives me the ticket to heaven where I'll walk the streets of gold and live in beautiful white mansions built in the clouds—oh yes! As I write this chapter, the vivid images I've had all my life of heaven and hell just pop into my head—exactly how my Sunday school teacher described them.

I was bent on making it to heaven, so I really wanted to be good. I tried so hard to be righteous. But I didn't realize this was also creating fear and guilt in me. As much as I desired to be perfect and righteous, I still made mistakes. I lived a typical example of the apostle Paul's words: the spirit is willing, but the thorn in my flesh is hindering me. And anytime I found myself in a situation that definitely was sin and not what God would approve of, I'd sink in guilt and fear of going to hell.

I'd beat myself up for making mistakes. I'd sink into endless prayers, begging God to forgive me and not reject me when he comes to take his select few to heaven. Sometimes this guilt would even affect my ability to serve in the church, as I'd hear a loud voice in my head telling me how I was unworthy of serving in the church of God even after genuinely repenting and praying to God to forgive my mistakes. Mind you, this wasn't a prompting of the Holy Spirit. It was more of a mockery from the enemy who laughed at me and reminded me of the bad things I did ten or fifteen years ago.

I really remember many times looking in the mirror and just seeing the person I was in my past and the person who made those mistakes. I just couldn't forgive myself for some of them, but they weren't even big things. They were simple things—genuine mistakes that I shouldn't be holding on to.

I didn't realize how much damage this caused me until I had a casual chat with a group of women about guilt. At that point I hadn't realized how much guilt I was holding on to. I didn't realize how much guilt was hindering me from loving myself and seeing myself as worthy. I didn't realize how judgmental I was of myself. This really bled into different areas of my life including my career, my ministry, and my relationships with others. No wonder I always felt like a fraud. I felt people wouldn't respect and accept me as their coach if they knew what I'd done in the past. I had a massive case of imposter syndrome.

Maybe you're like me and can identify with what I'm writing about here. Maybe you're holding on to your past and some mistakes you made, and this is making you see yourself as unlovable and unworthy. Maybe the enemy has been playing mind games with you and bringing up your past even though you're trying to live a better life. Maybe you feel like an imposter and a fraud. Maybe you feel the world is going to hate you if it finds out about what you did.

But today I want to urge you to forgive your past. Don't approach life from a fixed mindset. That makes things complicated. Approach life from a growth mindset. You learn as you grow. Stop being too hard on yourself for the mistakes you're making. Realize that each mistake is an opportunity to learn a lesson and evolve into the woman God wants you to be.

In addition to this, you are not your past. You are not your mistakes. What you did before you became born again was all wiped out when you accepted Christ as your personal Savior and you confessed with your mouth that he is the Lord of your life:

This means that anyone who belongs to Christ has become a new person. The old life is gone; a new life has begun! (2 Corinthians 5:17)

Stop wallowing in guilt for past mistakes. Life happens and we all make mistakes. Learn from your mistakes and just move on.

Start the journey to forgiving yourself by confessing to God and genuinely repenting from sin. If the sin is a habit or addiction that's hard to break away from, don't be afraid to seek help and reach out for help from Christian counselors, your pastor, mental health professionals, or coaches who can work with you to overcome this sin. But please give yourself a lot of self-compassion as you work on yourself. Remember, it's a journey, and God understands what you're going through. The God we serve is a loving and compassionate God. He knows our genuine struggles, so give yourself a lot of grace and compassion as you work on yourself. The fact that you have struggles doesn't mean you're not valuable. Remember, your worth is not on what you struggle with. You're worthy irrespective of your past mistakes.

Journal Activity

Am I holding on to any past mistakes?

_____

_____

_____

_____

_____

_____

_____

How am I defining my self-esteem by my past mistakes?

_____

_____

_____

_____

_____

_____

_____

_____

_____

Chapter Ten

STOP COMPARING YOURSELF TO OTHER PEOPLE

When I was growing up, I was a loud person. Anybody who knows Ama knows she's talkative. I'd talk so much in class that I'd get into trouble every time. I'd get reported. In my report cards, my teacher would always write, "She's talkative." I used to look down on myself so much because of it. I really wanted to be the quiet woman who wouldn't talk much. I tried so hard to fit myself into the image of the quiet woman.

But lo and behold, it turned out to be my biggest strength because I've been able to capitalize on talking a lot to develop my career as a coach, teacher, and a webinar instructor. I've been able to see the strength in something that used to get me into trouble.

One big hindrance for my self-love journey was that I couldn't stop comparing myself to others. I'd always look at other women on social media or even in my community and compare her life and achievements to mine, creating in me a lot of dissatisfaction. This included comparing myself to images of women on social media and in mass media, seeing the things I didn't have. I used people in my class who appeared calm, cool, and collected as the yardstick, and of course, every time I made a comparison, I found something another woman had that I didn't have, resulting in low self-esteem.

I always say that one of the biggest acts of disservice you can do to yourself as a woman is to compare yourself to other people. Comparing yourself to other people is different from admiring them. When you admire other people or other women, it's you seeing something good they're doing and acknowledging it without putting yourself down. It's about being able to say, "Oh, this is great. Yes, she's doing an awesome job, but that doesn't mean that I'm not good enough just because she's doing something I can't do."

When you compare yourself to other people, what happens is that you look at the strengths of other people. Then you beat yourself up and feel like you're not good enough because this person has something that you don't have or is doing something you don't get to do. When you compare yourself to people, you tend to look down on yourself. You think you're not good enough because they have something you don't have. However, when you admire others, you tend to see the good in them and celebrate their strengths while also celebrating yours.

If there's anything that I'm going to beg you to do, don't compare yourself to people. Just admire them. You're unique. Every woman has unique sets of skills, abilities, capabilities, strengths, and limitations. I've said this over and over again. When you see women on social media or TV who shine and use their strengths, don't look down on yourself, my dear. The best I can tell you is stop comparing yourself to them because they're showing you their strengths. You don't know what's behind those strengths. They also have their own weaknesses and other things they're dealing with as women. Every woman has her own can of worms. So please focus on your strengths and realize you're a unique woman with your own abilities. Focus on your strengths for success.

A lot of times, we women are busy thinking that certain character traits or certain things about us are weaknesses, while in reality they're actually things we could probably capitalize on for success. Focus on your uniqueness, as there may be just a few of you in this world with certain peculiarities. I always say different is better. The thing that makes you feel like you're different, bad, or not good enough is the thing you can use to become successful in life.

I always say God is a very interesting God because he made each of us special and unique. No woman on earth is the same.

Even twins are different. I'm a mom of identical twins. Genetically, they're supposed to be the same. But I'll tell you that even though they look the same from afar, you can see their character peculiarities when you get closer to them. Each one of these twins likes to eat different things and do other different activities. One of them is very calm and likes to do artistic stuff. The other one likes physical activities—running around and playing soccer. They're the same, but they're also different. I'm sharing this with you to make you realize that every woman is unique. You're unique in your own way. Stop comparing yourself to other people and focus on your strengths for success.

Chapter Eleven

AVOID TOXIC PEOPLE

"So encourage each other and build each other up, just as you are already doing." - 1 Thessalonians 5:11

The next key to developing a balanced self-esteem is to avoid toxic people and toxic relationships. In life you'll encounter different types of relationships and people. Some relationships are chosen for us, while we choose other relationships.

For example, we didn't get to decide which family we'd be born into. I always say if we all had a choice, we'd go for the richest families or the most prominent families in the world. But God decided who would be our mom and dad and who our siblings would be. Also, in the workplace, we don't have a choice on who becomes our coworker. The HR department hires people and forms a team that we belong to. They're in charge of that, and by default we have to work with these people as long as we're employed by the company. These are typical examples of a default relationship.

As time goes on, we encounter different people. We have a choice who we call our friends, who we marry, who we hang out with, or who we consider an acquaintance. These are all relationships of choice. If you have ever identified with being a people pleaser, follower, or codependent, you may notice that you mostly allow people to choose you instead of you choosing them.

This was the case with me growing up. The people I tried to make friends with were people who didn't like me for who I truly was. I'd put up a façade just to be accepted by them. This gave them so much power over me because I put the decision in their hands as though I wanted them to choose me by being willing to be what they'd like me to be.

This attracted a lot of toxic people into my life. If you've found yourself in a situation like that, then most likely you've faced so much rejection. As much as I'd tried to be chosen, I always felt rejected, as the choice would usually be short lived or turn into a toxic situation until I realized I could choose who I'd let into my life. When you exercise the power to choose who you engage with in relationships of choice, you can choose positive people.

Who Are Toxic People?

Toxic people are people who constantly talk about what's wrong with you. They never acknowledge what's good about you. Toxic people pollute the image you have of yourself and always make you feel like you're not good enough. If you engage a lot with toxic people, they make you focus on the bad. They affect your focus on who you are. Instead of focusing on your strengths and having a balanced view of yourself, they make you hyperfocus on what's not good about you. Toxic people are very dangerous. You want to stay away from them.

Toxic people usually feed off people who have low self-esteem. People with low self-esteem give too much power and control to toxic people. They twist themselves into a pretzel so they could be accepted by them and are willing to inconvenience themselves so they can be chosen by them. You'll know your relationships are toxic if the focus is always on what's wrong with you.

Choose Positive People

You want to hang out or surround yourself with positive people—people who like you for who you are. They're ready to accept your limitations and challenges. They love you for what's in you and not what's outside of you—

your money, social status, clothes, car, house, designer bags, degree, and position in life. Positive people give you constructive criticism. In positive relationships of choice, you have a mutual choice to be with each other. You bless each other, love each other, and help each other to become better. It's a partnership.

Positive people aren't fake. They're able to acknowledge what's good about you and when something is wrong. They don't just say, "Oh, you're perfect." When they correct you, they correct you in love, trying to help you to become a better person. They allow you to work on yourself so you can become a better person, not to make you feel bad or not good enough. Positive people are the people you want to associate with.

My dear reader, with this insight, you want to shift from only being chosen to also becoming a chooser. Choose wisely who will be your inner circle. Choose wisely who you allow to speak into your life. Choose wisely who you associate with. Don't just give power to others. You also have the power to choose your relationships. Be in mutual agreements, not toxic one-sided engagements.

You need to choose people and be chosen by them to build a healthy relationship with them. Of course, you'll each make some compromises as you build your relationship. However, if you choose people who want you to become a far-too-diluted version of your true self before they can choose you back, then you probably have to reconsider your choice. It may just not be a good fit.

Journal Activity

Do I choose my circle or do I let them choose me?

_____

_____

_____

_____

_____

_____

_____

How have I given too much power to the people in my inner circle?

_____

_____

_____

_____

_____

_____

_____

_____

_____

_____

Chapter Twelve

CHOOSE PROGRESS OVER PERFECTION

"I don't mean to say that I have already achieved these things or that I have already reached perfection. But I press on to possess that perfection for which Christ Jesus first possessed me. 13 No, dear brothers and sisters, I have not achieved it,[a] but I focus on this one thing: Forgetting the past and looking forward to what lies ahead, 14 I press on to reach the end of the race and receive the heavenly prize for which God, through Christ Jesus, is calling us."
-Philippians 3:12-14

A client of mine reached out to me the other day. She was upset because she had her daughter three years ago and has still not been able to bounce back after gaining weight. She said one of the celebrities she follows on Instagram just had a baby and did a bikini photoshoot showing her body that bounced back in three months.

To give you a bit of background, this client started her wellness journey with me three months ago. From a coaching standpoint, she's making significant progress and is taking baby steps toward her goal every day. But the biggest challenge this client had was that she was so focused on what she didn't have that she couldn't celebrate her wins. This always created pressure for her, as she overstretched herself and beat herself, which only drowned her in low self-esteem and dissatisfaction.

Becoming a balanced self-lover empowers you to let go of the need to be perfect in everything. Like my client, the high achiever and perfectionist in me also give me so much pressure sometimes. When I reach for a goal, sometimes it's all or nothing, leading to a lot of dissatisfaction and stress. I realize that when my focus is on what I don't have or how far away I am from my goal, I become very dissatisfied. I feel I'm not good enough. I feel I'm a loser and a failure. However, when my focus is on what I have and how far I've come in reaching my goal, I'm more at peace. I feel more encouraged and motivated to keep moving forward. Anxiety is lessened and depression has no space in my life when I'm focused on the half-full cup.

When we seek perfection, it's mostly because we want to stand out, have external validation, or value ourselves by the perfect things we achieve or do. But this need and pressure to be perfect only sink us into the pit of dissatisfaction, low self-esteem, and feelings of unworthiness.

This pressure to be perfect is fueled by social media images these days. We all post pictures that have been edited with the world's best filter apps. When we see each other's posts, we just see perfection, which is far removed from reality. We forget that we're all showing up with our best foot forward. We're not telling the dirty side of our stories. My dear reader, no woman is perfect. We're all dealing with something and have our own challenges. The only perfect entity is the God we serve. He's the only one who can be called perfect. Even the things that exist here on earth have their own flaws depending on your point of view.

So please focus on progress, not perfection. Learn to look at the glass half full instead of half empty. Learn to celebrate your little wins. Learn to be focused on how much closer you're getting to your goal instead of how far you are from it.

Journal Activity

How do I operate in the "All or nothing" rule?

_____

_____

_____

_____

_____

_____

_____

How beneficial will it be to look at the
glass half full instead of half empty?

_____

_____

_____

_____

_____

_____

_____

_____

_____

_____

Chapter Thirteen

LIVE A VALUE-BASED LIFE, NOT A GOAL-BASED LIFE

Three friends were walking into an arboretum. This arboretum had very beautiful trees and the most exotic varieties of flowers and other plants. Along the path that led to this oasis of beautiful plants were some very colorful, beautiful roses. They were indeed a gem to experience.

Miss G, the first of the three friends, didn't even notice the roses that were lined up on the path. She was really in a rush. She was so focused on the ultimate destination that she couldn't even experience this opportunity of a lifetime along the path to the ultimate destination.

Miss S immediately noticed the roses along the path and stopped to enjoy them. She got sucked into enjoying those rose petals and their beautiful smell to the point that she forgot about the arboretum, which had even better things to witness. She just stood there and didn't get to experience the arboretum.

Miss V was the third friend. She also noticed the rose petals. She stopped intermittently to enjoy the roses that were lined across the path but still made an effort to keep moving forward. She continued walking the path as she admired the roses until she made it to the arboretum where she had an even better experience.

Which of these three women—Miss Goals, Miss Stuck, and Miss Values, respectively—do you think had the best experience on this journey?

Miss Goals is like the woman so focused on her goals that she doesn't enjoy the journey toward them. She's the high achiever who stretches herself too thin and overstretches herself to achieve her goal. She wraps her life around her goals. She achieves these goals but still doesn't feel worthy or valuable because her goals are an ever-shifting target. The more things she achieves, the higher the target. Women like Miss Goals look accomplished on the outside but have a lot of internal turmoil and feelings of worthlessness. They're goal driven but not enjoying the journey to achieving their goals.

Miss Stuck got to the path that led to her goal of getting into the arboretum. She noticed the roses but lost focus and just stayed with them. She got stuck on her path to her goal. She knew where she wanted to get to in the beginning. She also loved the experience with the roses, but that distracted her so much that she lost track of why she even walked that path in the first place. Women like Miss Stuck can't make any progress because they're fixated on and complacent in the few wins they had.

Miss Values had a great experience. She noticed and enjoyed the roses but kept focusing on her goals. She didn't rush. She took her time to savor the whole walking experience until she reached her goal of entering the arboretum.

As you read about these three friends, which one of these friends do you think you can identify with the most? Are you Miss Goals who's more goal driven and can't even enjoy her journey to success? Are you Miss Stuck who easily loses focus and feels like she has failed and isn't worthy in the end? Are you Miss Values who knows what her goals are but also makes sure she lives a life that fulfills her values while she journeys into success?

If you're like me, then probably you have so many goals you're trying to achieve. Some of these goals are so big that they require a lot of effort, energy, and time on your part to achieve them. I usually find myself being like Miss Goals. I usually put so much pressure on myself to the point where successes aren't even enjoyable. As soon as I've achieved success, I can't celebrate it because I'm so focused on the next big thing.

My dear reader, let's aim to live a value-based life. Values are our core beliefs. They usually guide us into making the right choices and taking the right directions in life. Values inform us about what's most important to us. When we're in touch with our values, we can make the right choices and make the right decisions so we can serve our intrinsic needs.

Let's aim to enjoy life while we strive for success. Let's aim to not put pressure on ourselves for nothing. Let's not be lackadaisical in our ways for the sake of taking it easy. Rather, let's take life one step at a time, ensuring that we can celebrate our journey of life. With a value-based lifestyle, our self-esteem isn't wrapped in the goals we're aiming to achieve or the goals we didn't achieve. With a value-based lifestyle, we see goals as important, but we focus more on our inner fulfillment and what's most important to us. A value-based life is important if you want to become a balanced self-lover.

Journal Activity

Which of these three women do I identify with?

_____

_____

_____

_____

_____

_____

_____

_____

How will a value based life impact my life?

_____

_____

_____

_____

_____

_____

_____

_____

_____

Chapter Fourteen

MAINTAIN A BALANCED SELF-ESTEEM IN TRYING TIMES

As you embark on this self-love journey, seasons of life will definitely continue to exist. Life happens. Sometimes you may think you have life all planned out, have your goals in place, and everything seems perfect. Then out of the blue, something just happens and all you've worked hard for just comes crumbling down on you. This feeling is so disappointing, confusing, and shocking. We've all been there before. It could be you or a loved one getting sick, death of a loved one, a job loss, bankruptcy, divorce or the end of a committed relationship, and so on. We just don't see it coming, and it just hits us as a big surprise.

Life threw a curveball at me a couple of years ago. I was pregnant with my twins. I was so excited about it because I'd always loved twins and wanted to have a set for myself. Then one morning I went for my twenty-week prenatal appointment. My doctor looked me in the eye and said to me that I was in a critical situation. I could either lose my babies, or I'd have them, but they might be so frail that they'd need the NICU to thrive.

This was so hard on me. I just couldn't believe that something that was a dream for me was now life threatening. Fast forward—I had my babies. They ended up in the NICU. They needed some surgeries and other special medical attention, but they thrived.

When we are going through tough times, it's very easy for us to feel like we're being punished for something we did wrong. That's exactly how I felt when I was going through this tough time. Sometimes I thought, "Why am I going through this? What have I done wrong? Am I cursed? Is there something wrong with me?" Honestly, my self-esteem just dwindled. On a scale of one to ten, I'd say I was in the negatives. I gave up on life and on myself. I looked down on myself and felt like all hope was lost.

It was a tough time that I thought would never end. But today I look back and see that this experience wasn't easy, but it has increased my faith in God. It has also built greater strength and resilience in me than I had before. I learned some lessons from that tough, distressful situation. I want to share this with you because I know that as you go on this self-love journey, you may be faced with life experiences that may make you lose focus and feel bad about yourself.

Here are four practical tips to continue to maintain a balanced self-esteem if you're faced with tough times and stressful situations:

1. Find your strength in God. The number one practical way you can feel good about yourself during tough times is to find your strength in God. Let him be your source of hope and joy. When you have tried all the possibilities to overcome your situation and none of them has worked, just turn to him. Even when all people forsake you, he never forsakes you. He says when you go through the valley of the shadow of death, he is with you. He will never leave you nor forsake you. He will work everything out for your good as long as you depend on him. Develop a relationship with him. Give it all to him. Let him have his way in your life. Surrender your will to him, and he will come through for you no matter how long it takes.

2. Avoid defining your self-esteem by your current situation. When I was going through my tough pregnancy, one of the biggest mistakes I made was defining my self-esteem by what I was going through. I felt so low and thought I wasn't good enough. Until I switched from defining my self-esteem by my situation, I just kept sinking in self-pity.

Don't make the same mistake that I made. You're going through tough times, but it doesn't change who you are or what you're worth. Your situation changed, but your worth didn't change. Don't define your self-esteem by your situation.

Define your self-esteem by who God says you are. This is a practical way you can feel good about yourself during tough times.

3. Watch your thoughts and think positively. Feel good about yourself during tough times by thinking positively. See your situation as a transition that will pass. Nothing is permanent. Life happens and your situation will change.

Don't just give up on life. Pick up yourself and start afresh. Don't stay down because life throws a curveball at you. Your circumstances are temporary and will turn around before you know it.

If you think positive and look at the positives of what you are going through, it allows you to not lose hope, and it strengthens you so you won't give up on yourself.

4. Get the right support system in place. When life throws a curveball at you, another practical way to feel good about yourself is to get the right support system in place. Surround yourself with the right people— people who speak positivity into your life situation, who encourage you, and who don't give up on you because you're going through tough times.

Know that you're not an island. You can't go it alone. You need emotional and psychological support. Sometimes you also need physical support. Don't put on a brave face and pretend nothing is happening in your world. Putting up a façade is only going to hurt you more.

Don't be afraid to ask for help from people around you. You need people in your life that you feel safe with so you can share what you're actually feeling inside. You can consider trusted family and friends, therapists, counselors, and life coaches—just to mention a few.

In a nutshell, tough times come and go, but when you find yourself in tough times, use the above four keys to help you maintain a balanced self-esteem. The more confident you are, the stronger you will be to overcome your situation and bounce back.

WRAP-UP

In this part of the book, I've discussed the different strategies and keys for developing a balanced self-esteem and becoming a balanced self-lover. I've also shared resources on how to feel good about yourself in bad times. This is very important because as you go through this self-love journey, things will definitely happen, and you want to keep the momentum going without losing hope and focus.

Depending on where you are with your self-love journey, you may already be using some of these strategies. Some of them may be new to you. I hope all the things I've discussed in this section will come in handy depending on what you need at the moment.

I must tell you that some may seem more relevant depending on times and seasons of your life. Maybe you feel overwhelmed by all this information. Or maybe you really love the information, but you don't know where to begin. You feel a sense of confusion on how to start applying all the information and resources shared in this book. Don't worry. I have a plan for you. The next section will walk you through implementing these resources into your life so you can start your journey to becoming a balanced self-lover.

Part Three

JUMPSTART YOUR JOURNEY TODAY

In this part of the book, we'll delve into the application of the information and strategies to your life. There are a lot of journal prompts to walk you into beginning your journey or continuing from where you were before you reached out for this book. As you go through this part of the book, you may find out some truths that are hard to confront and deal with. Please take it one day at a time. Don't be too hard on yourself. My prayer is that God will guide you into the healing He has for you so this self-love journey will be a fruitful and successful one.

Chapter Fifteen

WHAT HAPPENED TO YOU?

The first thing I want to urge you to do is to answer the question: what happened to you? You may recall that I've mentioned labels—people pleaser, follower, drama queen, and overachiever—at the beginning of this book. Those labels don't just appear. They are usually placed on people because of some behaviors or actions that may have warranted them.

I also answered this simple but important question at a point in my self-love journey. It helped me discover the root cause of my insecurities and why I identified so much with those labels. I started out thinking back as far as I could remember about what happened that pivoted me into the road of insecurities. And yes, I did find out about a lot of things that happened to me, which I didn't know were fueling my struggles as an adult.

I discovered that my struggles with self-esteem were birthed by childhood trauma. This included an incident at the age of eight. As I looked back on it, I realized how simple and insignificant the experience was, but my eight-year-old brain didn't process it the way I process it today as an adult. There was a miscommunication between a group of friends and me, which made them gang up on me, scold me, and beat me up. Honestly, I laugh about the incident today. Now I see it as little kids fighting. But my eight-year-old brain processed it as "I am not good enough." I thought no one would choose me to be their friend if I didn't try hard enough to be liked and accepted by them. I thought everyone hated me. I thought people would always gang up on me because I wasn't good enough. I lived with this trauma for more than twenty years of my life, leading me into toxic friendships and relationships because I felt I needed to do anything possible to be chosen by others.

I never realized how much this incident had influenced the toxic patterns I found myself in. It caused fear of rejection and fear of being left out. This had influenced my need for belonging, acceptance, and validation, which made me a people pleaser who always felt used by others.

As I look back to my life, I realize that all the years of people pleasing, being unable to say no, and inconveniencing myself just to be liked and validated by people were rooted in that emotional wound and the limiting beliefs that came with it. I always felt I wasn't good enough and something was wrong with me.

My dear reader, I'm sharing this with you not because I'm looking for pity. I just want you to realize that healing is possible if we put in the work. Experiences that we faced from the day we were born have a huge influence on how we value ourselves. Yes, we have our own genetic makeup, but the environment and circumstances earlier in life go a long way to affect us all our lives. The sooner you deal with why you are who you are today, the better it will be for you on this self-love journey.

In this chapter, you want to answer the simple question: what happened to you? But wait a minute! Maybe you're afraid to do this because you know there's something and you're afraid to confront it. I know you may have bottled up some of these past experiences because they hurt so badly. Anytime you take a step closer to confronting them, you're flooded with so much unbearable emotion. That's to be expected, but this is a very important exercise that will help you identify the root cause of your insecurities and challenges with your self-worth and self-love.

It's possible to heal from past hurts and emotional wounds. But it first starts with you asking yourself, "What happened to me?" and looking inward to find the root cause of your insecurities. You can do this. Just start small and ask God for insight into the root cause of your woes. Let these journal prompts guide you into exploring what happened to you and the reason for what you're facing today. That's the first step in dealing with your insecurities and becoming a balanced self-lover.

Journal Activity

How was your childhood like?

_____

_____

_____

_____

How did you experience any trauma that
probably has influenced how you treat yourself
today and feel about yourself today?

_____

_____

_____

_____

_____

Have you been through any life experiences
that affect your level of self-love today?

_____

_____

_____

_____

_____

Are there past mistakes that you can't let go of?

_____

_____

_____

_____

_____

_____

Are there past hurts and offenses you cannot forgive?

_____

_____

_____

_____

_____

_____

Did you lose a loved one who you
haven't been able to let go?

_____

_____

_____

_____

_____

_____

Chapter Sixteen

GOD IS CALLING YOU TO HEAL

"...Come to me, all of you who are weary and carry heavy burdens, and I will give you rest. Take my yoke upon you. Let me teach you, because I am humble and gentle at heart, and you will find rest for your souls. For my yoke is easy to bear, and the burden I give you is light."

-Matthew 11:28–30

*N*ow that you have identified or acknowledged what happened to you and have an idea what influenced the acquisition of your so-called labels, we want to take it a step further.

My dear reader, God is calling you to heal. I know you may be afraid of confronting these past traumatic experiences, but I can reassure you that the earlier you start your healing journey, the better it would be for you to move forward in your self-love journey. Sometimes what we're so afraid of is usually the thing that we need to confront to make progress. Would you rather face the fear now and have long-term healing, or would you rather avoid it and let it bleed for the rest of your life?

It's like having a sore on your arm that's oozing with pus, but you've covered it with a bandage. You're so afraid to rip the bandage off and get the sore treated by a doctor who can put the right antibiotics on it so that it can heal properly and be gone for good. Every day you're protecting it, though it's painful and itching. It causes you so much discomfort to the point where it's eating into different parts of your body. You're developing fevers and headaches. They're affecting your mood. All of this is caused by one sore that you're refusing to treat. Would you rather live with this infected sore that can develop into something worse, or would you rather rip off the bandage and treat it so you can enjoy a sore-free future? The same applies to our emotional wounds. The more we bottle them up, the worse they get and the more they eat into other areas of our lives including our self-love and our self-esteem.

After discovering the root cause of my insecurities, I went to counseling to do the work and heal from that particular trauma and other traumas that were influencing my insecurities. I realized that until I recognized and started my healing journey from the traumas, the toxic patterns would continue because I needed that validation. I was stuck in a pattern where I'd ignore the people around me who genuinely loved me and were kind to me. I'd get so obsessed with trying to be accepted by people who weren't emotionally available or who were toxic and didn't value me for me.

My dear reader, God is calling you to heal. He has the power to heal you. You use sugar, nicotine, coffee, pornography, alcohol, narcotics, and other things to ease the pain, but long-lasting healing and peace can only be offered by God. Let him turn your pain and wounds into testimonies. Let him transform you from victim to victor. Let him heal you so you can have long-lasting peace. Turn that trauma and pain over to him. Surrender them all to him and let him have his way in your life. Depend on him to direct your path as you go through this healing process.

However, as you depend on God to heal your past wounds, sometimes they're so deep that we need to reach out for support from others as we work on healing ourselves. Yes, sometimes we can't go it alone. If you do find something traumatic and hard to deal with by yourself, I urge you to reach out to a trained professional Christian counselor, mental health coach, or therapist to help you work through those past traumas. This is how you can build a solid self-esteem that's not built on pain and trauma but on a truly whole and healed person.

Journal Activity

Write God a letter, turning your trauma
and pain over to him and surrendering
them all to him to help you heal.

_____

_____

_____

_____

_____

_____

_____

_____

_____

_____

_____

_____

_____

_____

_____

_____

_____

_____

_____

_____

Chapter Seventeen

FOUR-STEP SELF-ESTEEM BOOSTER

Now that you have answered the question of what happened to you and you have started your healing, I want to introduce you to the four-step self-esteem booster. This is a very powerful exercise that will give you perspective on your strengths and weaknesses. This short activity is going to help you boost your self-esteem. It's going to help you realize the things about you that are good and learn to love them and focus on them. It's going to help you realize the things about you that you can actually work on and become better at as well as the things that may never change that you need to learn to live with and accept.

Sometimes we're so busy fighting with what we honestly and genuinely have no control over. A lot of the weaknesses we're fighting and beating ourselves up for are usually things that may never change. We need to accept them as they are. This exercise will help you refocus and come to the realization of where you need to focus your energy as you work on becoming your best self.

As much as we want to love ourselves just as we are, we don't want to become stagnant. Growth is very important for you physically, mentally, and emotionally. You want to become better and better each day, but you need to be clear on the things that you can work on and change. This exercise is great at helping you do that so you can focus your energy and efforts on the right thing.

Journal Activity

Step one. What are the things you love about yourself? What are the things you perceive as your strengths? Write a list of all the things—as many as you can think about—that you love about yourself.

_____

_____

_____

_____

_____

_____

_____

Step two. What are the things you don't love about yourself? What are your perceived weaknesses? What are the things you hate about yourself? Write them down.

_____

_____

_____

_____

_____

_____

_____

Step three. Now that we have a list of your strengths and weaknesses, break those weaknesses into two sets:

What are the weaknesses beyond your scope of influence? What are the weaknesses you can never change?

_____

_____

_____

_____

_____

_____

_____

What are the weaknesses you can change—the ones you can work on and become better at?

_____

_____

_____

_____

_____

_____

_____

Step four. Write a decision letter. I want you to write a letter to yourself telling yourself that you're going to play up your strengths. You're going to work on the weaknesses you can work on. You're going to learn to live with the weaknesses that you know can never change or may never change in your lifetime.

_____

_____

_____

_____

_____

_____

_____

_____

_____

_____

_____

_____

_____

_____

_____

_____

_____

_____

Chapter Eighteen

BE TRANSFORMED BY THE RENEWING OF YOUR MIND

S elf-love is an ongoing journey. As much as we know that we're valuable and God loves us, sometimes we forget and lose focus, especially in times of transition, times of panic, or tragic times. In this chapter, I'm sharing with you my personal self-esteem and self-love affirmations from the Bible that I use to remind myself constantly when I'm going through tough times.

As you continue your journey to becoming a balanced self-lover, you can use these affirmations to remind yourself daily what the Bible says about you. You can post them in conspicuous spots in your home, work, car, or other everyday locations.

The more you speak these words to yourself, the more it gets registered in your mind and sticks with you. You can even record them in an audio format and play it over and over again—as many times as you can. You may not believe them in the beginning, but I can assure you that your mind will be renewed as you do this exercise:

As Romans 12:2 says, don't copy the behavior and customs of this world, but let God transform you into a new person by changing the way you think. Then you will learn to know God's will for you, which is good, pleasing, and perfect.

As you meditate on the word of God and soak in what God says about you and who he says you are, you'll see your mind and your toxic beliefs transform. The way you think changes, and you'll get closer to God, believing in his will and purpose for your life. At that point your definition of your self-worth won't be based on social media images, what the world says about you, or what labels have been placed on you in the past. Your worth won't be defined by your past, what traumatic experience you faced, or what mistakes you made. Your worth won't be defined by your financial worth, your educational degree, your physical features, or your marital status. Your worth will be built on the solid rock of the word of God and who God says you are.

WRAP-UP

In this part of the book, I've walked you through the steps to starting your self-love journey. Whether you're now starting your journey or you've already started but are feeling stuck, the practical exercises and journal prompts in this part of the book will help you refocus and start from somewhere.

Outro

YOU CAN DO THIS!

In this book I've prepared you for your self-love journey by giving you simple but effective strategies you can implement in your everyday life so you can develop a balanced self-esteem and begin to see yourself as God sees you.

I'm so proud of you for making it to the end of this book. I'm sure your head is spinning from all the information, but you don't have to do it all at once. Take this journey one day at a time. Start small and take baby steps until your self-love tank starts to overflow and extend to others.

Don't rush your transformation. Please don't be too hard on yourself. Whenever you feel like giving up, just remember that you can do all things through Christ who strengthens you. Time will come when you think you're not making any progress, but just don't give up and keep pushing. God will work it all out for good.

I want to encourage you to be grateful for every little win. The journey to becoming a balanced self-lover is a long one, so please take it one step at a time and learn to celebrate every step closer to your ultimate goal.

I'll be thrilled to hear about your self-love journey and how this book has blessed you. Send me a message at www.empoweredforbalance.com/contact. I also invite you to join the Balanced Dame Newsletter to get support and more strategies as you go on this self-love journey at https://www.empoweredforbalance.com/burnout.

ABOUT THE AUTHOR

Ama Brew is an author, an ICF certified coach, a keynote speaker, and a human resources consultant. Combining her BA in psychology and a master's degree in organizational leadership and human resource management as well as life coach training and personal experience, Ama delivers a personalized coaching experience to help her life coaching clients gain more control in their lives, achieve balance, and design the lives they were meant to live—fulfilled, confident, joyful, and free from what has been holding them back.

Following a rewarding career as a human resources manager, Ama started a childcare business to be fully involved in the daily care of her children. She became so committed to their care that she lost herself for years.

Ama found her way back to a balanced and purposeful life and is now on a mission to help other women who are experiencing the taxing demands of balancing motherhood, caring for a home, and a professional life.

Ama founded and developed Empowered for Balance for that purpose and works with women who are spinning multiple plates and looking for more fulfillment, purpose, and balance in their lives. Ama delves into the root cause of the imbalance in her client's lives to educate, empower, and coach them to transform so they too can live more balanced and purposeful lives.

Ama supports her husband in pastoring a church in New Hampshire, USA. She and her husband are parents to a beautiful daughter and two adorable twin boys.

Connect with Ama at the following links:
https://www.empoweredforbalance.com/
https://www.facebook.com/empoweredforbalance/
https://www.instagram.com/empoweredforbalance/
https://www.pinterest.com/empoweredforbalance/

OTHER BOOKS IN THE SERIES!!!

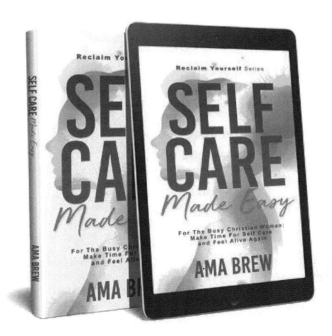

Understanding Self Care and creating a sustainable Self Care routine so you can eliminate burnout and live stress free

Grab Your Paperback, E-book or Audio Copy Now on Amazon!!
https://www.empoweredforbalance.com/selfcarebook

Made in the USA
Middletown, DE
02 November 2021